FLASH WISDOM

A Curated Collection of Mind-Blowing,
Perspective-Changing Quotes

RUSS KICK

 **disinformation**®

Published by:
Disinformation Books
An imprint of Red Wheel/Weiser, LLC
With offices at
665 Third Street, Suite 400
San Francisco, CA 94107
www.redwheelweiser.com

Library of Congress Cataloging-in-Publication Data

Flash wisdom : a curated collection of mind-blowing, perspective-changing,
and eye-opening quotes / [edited by] Russ Kick.
     pages cm
 Summary: "This book collects surprising, jolting, discomforting, and comforting
insights into living a full, unbridled life, questioning authority and reality, relating
to fellow humans, creating, risking, loving, living with uncertainty, and staying
sane in an insane world"-- Provided by publisher.
  ISBN 978-1-938875-12-0 (paperback)
  1. Conduct of life--Quotations, maxims, etc. 2. Wisdom--Quotations, maxims,
etc. I. Kick, Russell, editor of compilation.
  PN6084.C556F62 2015
  081--dc23   2014041758

Cover design by Jim Warner
Cover photograph: Books on Books, 2003 (w/c on paper), Wolstenholme,
Jonathan (b.1950) / Private Collection /
© Portal Painters / Bridgeman Images
Typeset by Kathryn Sky-Peck
Typeset in Sabon

Printed in Canada
MAR
10 9 8 7 6 5 4 3 2 1

CONTENTS

INTRODUCTION

> A quotation at the right moment
> is like bread to the famished.
>
> —Talmud

> A book that furnishes no quotations is,
> *me judice*, no book—it is a plaything.
>
> —Thomas Love Peacock

I'm a quotation junkie. Growing up surrounded by books, I gravitated to the quote collections on the family bookshelves, including the doorstoppers *The International Dictionary of Thought* and *The Great Quotations* (the latter compiled in the 1960s by the great investigative journalist George Seldes). When I was at my grandparents' house, I'd turn to the "Quotable Quotes" section of *Reader's Digest*. Whenever an issue of *The Sun* is within reach, I head to the last page, "Sunbeams," a collection of quotes, usually on that issue's theme.

I also like lists, bullet points, fortune-cookie fortunes, bumper stickers, Dr. Bronner's soap labels, flash cards, microfiction, trivia books. I prefer short stories to novels, short films to feature films, haiku and quatrains to five-page poems, Hemingway to Joyce. Maybe that's why I drink spirits, not wine or beer. Distill things for me. Boil them down to their essences. Take out the dross, the impurities, the filler.

I like wisdom that way, too. I probably don't have time for an 800-page treatise on the intricate meaning of life, the universe, and everything. Don't make me wait for that epiphany. Give me your insight in an instant.

• • •

The best quotes are the ones that crystallize a truth, that offer a new way of seeing things, or that point out something that you've always known even though the thought has never fully formed in your mind. Suddenly, there it is on the page. In a compact form. Your perspective shifts.

This effect has long been noted with regard to books. The great 20th-century novelist and essayist James Baldwin said: "You read something which you thought only happened to you, and you discover that it happened 100 years ago to Dostoevsky. This is a very great liberation for the suffering, struggling person, who always thinks that he is alone."

Excellent quotations offer the same thing—the same sense of connection, the same insight into the human condition—in a tiny format, much easier to encounter and quicker to absorb than a book.

$$\bullet \ \ \bullet \ \ \bullet$$

That concision is undoubtedly the biggest selling point of quotes, maxims, aphorisms, and proverbs. Easy to ingest. Easy to remember. Available to interject into a conversation at a moment's notice. You can sprinkle them throughout your own writing or talks and lectures, tape them to your bathroom mirror, use them to sign off your emails (in your "sig line"), tweet them....

The rise of social media has led to a resurgence in the quoting of quotes. Twitter, with its limit of 140 characters, is a natural habitat for quotations. Facebook doesn't have a hard-and-fast maximum, but it does reward brevity. Both sites allow posting of small images, and those images are often quotations, usually accompanied by or overlaying a photo. These sites are chockablock with quotations from the past 3,000 years.

While social networks, JPEGs, and email sig lines provide the ideal platform for short bits of text, people's love of quotations goes way back. Lifting one, two, or three sentences (occasionally more) out of a much larger text and pinning it to a new page like a butterfly is a millennia-long pursuit. In his book *The Words of Others: From Quotations to Culture*, Northwestern University professor Gary Saul Morson reveals that collections of quotations existed in ancient times; they were especially popular in the Middle Ages and the Renaissance; the first book printed in Britain was, in fact, a compendium of quotations from the great philosophers. John Bartlett—the 19th-century bookseller whose name has become synonymous with quotation collections—was actually taking part in a long tradition.

• • •

So what do I look for in quotations? How did I select the ones for *Flash Wisdom*?

I started with my favorites, the ones that have moved me the most through the years. Helen Schucman on the overriding importance not of seeking love but of tearing down our internal barriers against it. André Gide's exhortation: "Believe those who are seeking the truth. Doubt those who find it." Thoreau on the true price of anything ("the amount of life you exchange for it"). Leonard Cohen on acceptance ("If you don't become the ocean you'll be seasick every day."), and Chuck Palahniuk on materialism ("The things you own end up owning you."). Pablo Neruda's 1924 declaration/offer to his lover—"I want to do with you what spring does with the cherry trees."—which I'm told is still being used by Lotharios throughout South America. Bruce Lee's stirring reminder: "In great attempts it is glorious even to fail." Yoko Ono's surprisingly difficult instruction: "Try to say nothing negative about anybody for three days, for forty-five days, for three months. See what happens to your life." The harsh medicine offered by a bumper-sticker I saw around twenty years ago: "The only common denominator in all your fucked-up relationships is you." William Blake's support of "the road of excess," and George Eliot's note of hope to those of us who are no longer spring chickens: "It is never too late to be what you might have been."

From there, I started buying and checking out quotation books by the armful. I dove into the bottomless pit that is Wikiquote. I asked people I know for the quotes that mean the most to them. I found gems that I'd forgotten, and discovered loads more that resonated with me. Not that I'm convinced that every quotation I selected is the truth (whatever that is). Many seem to hit the proverbial nail on the head. Others are obvious overstatements, but they contain enough truth to be worth pondering. A handful might even be completely wrongheaded . . . but they make points that I can't easily dismiss.

I banished the twee, the clichéd, the cynical, the too-clever. You might disagree, of course. One person's treasure is another person's twaddle. I tried to stick with the most eloquent, the punchiest, the most honest, and/or the most insightful and revealing.

Because of quotations in this book, I've changed my outlook on life, or at least certain aspects of it. I've put new approaches into practice. I look at other people and their actions in different ways.

• • •

Many of the best quotes are like the best poems: they point to a truth, but they don't spell it out. You get an insight, but it's up to you to figure out what to do with it, how to implement it. Take this quote from Dostoevsky: "Much unhappiness has come into the world because of bewilderment and things left unsaid." I hear this as a call to speak important things, and to speak them clearly, to people who are important to us. But how exactly do we do this? He doesn't tell us. Obviously we can't say literally everything that's unsaid . . . none of us would be silent for even a moment. This titan of Russian literature is implying that a few crucial things are going unsaid. What those things are, and how and when to say them . . . well, that's up to each of us to decide.

A small number of these quotes, however, do offer explicit advice. Sylvia Plath recommends hot baths as a panacea for whatever ails us, physically or emotionally. Hemingway commands us to shut up and truly listen to other people. Napoleon advises us to never make promises.

Taking the opposite approach, a tiny portion of these *bon mots* are highly abstract. Octavio Paz's meditation on the nature of the romantic couple ("the point of intersection of all forces and the seed of all forms") comes to mind. As does J. Krishnamurti's famous, defining statement: "Truth is a pathless land."

The vast majority of quotes in this book, though, sprawl over the spectrum between concrete, actionable advice and mystical obliqueness.

• • •

If a light going on in someone's eyes has ever literally happened, then I saw it happen at a garden party. A community activist was there—a builder of metaphorical bridges—so I relayed a Lincoln quote: "Am I not destroying my enemies when I make friends of them?" There was a pause. I could see him processing. Then he smiled hugely, his eyes sparkling. "Ahhh. Yes!"

I know that feeling well. Here's hoping it happens at least once to each reader of this book.

—Russ Kick

You read something which you thought only
happened to you, and you discover that it
happened 100 years ago to Dostoevsky.
This is a very great liberation for the
suffering, struggling person, who always
thinks that he is alone.
This is why art is important.

—James Baldwin

REALITY, TRUTH, AND SUCH THINGS

LET'S BEGIN AT THE BEGINNING, the foundation for everything else. Well . . . let's try, at least. Before we look at living and loving, creating and crying, sex and death, family and government, let's see if we can get a bead on reality, existence, truth—the substrate from which everything forms. This topic always ungrounds me. My head spins. How do I know anything? How would I know even if I did happen to know something? How am I managing to make the slightest bit of sense out of the chaotic jumble of atoms (or whatever) that (I think) surrounds me? Do I even exist? If you think I'm exaggerating, pollinate your brain with the following barrage of thoughts and observations from chemists, physicists, philosophers, poets, sages, magical realist writers, and other reality hackers. Who needs psychedelics to get to altered states?

The opposite of a true statement is a false statement, but the opposite of a profound truth may well be another profound truth.

—Niels Bohr (paraphrased)

We don't see things as they are, we see them as we are.

—Anaïs Nin

Reality is frequently **inaccurate.**

—Douglas Adams

Since the initial publication
of the chart of the
electromagnetic spectrum, **humans
have learned**
that what they can
touch, smell, see, and hear is

less than one-millionth of reality.

—R. Buckminster Fuller

Civilised life, you know, is based on a huge number
of illusions in which we all collaborate willingly. The
trouble is we forget after a while that they are illusions,
and we are deeply shocked when reality is torn down
around us.

—J. G. Ballard

Everything we see hides another thing; we always want
to see what is hidden by what we see.

—René Magritte

Everybody gets so much information all day long that
they lose their common sense.

—Gertrude Stein

A hallucination is **a species of reality.**

—Terence McKenna

Outside is pure energy and colorless substance. All of the rest happens through the mechanism of our senses. Our eyes see just a small fraction of the light in the world. It is a trick to make a colored world, which does not exist outside of human beings.

—Albert Hofmann

If the doors of perception were cleansed, everything would appear to man as it is: infinite.

—William Blake

We are more closely connected to the invisible than to the visible.

—Novalis

Reality is nothing but a collective hunch.

—Lily Tomlin and Jane Wagner

Our normal waking consciousness, rational consciousness as we call it, is but one special type of consciousness, whilst all about it, parted from it by the filmiest of screens, there lie potential forms of consciousness entirely different. We may go through life without suspecting their existence; but apply the requisite stimulus, and at a touch they are there in all their completeness. . . . They forbid a premature closing of our accounts with reality.

—William James

It is inconceivable that anything should be existing.

—Celia Green

In studying the literature connected with my work,
I became aware of the great universal significance of
visionary experience. It plays a dominant role, not only
in mysticism and the history of religion, but also in the
creative process in art, literature, and science. More
recent investigations have shown that many persons also
have visionary experiences in daily life, though most of
us fail to recognize their meaning and value. Mystical
experiences, like those that marked my childhood, are
apparently far from rare.

—Albert Hofmann

About half of the U.S. public (49%) says they have had a religious or mystical experience, defined as a "moment of sudden religious insight or awakening." This is similar to a survey conducted in 2006 but much higher than in surveys conducted in 1976 and 1994, and more than twice as high as in a 1962 Gallup survey (22%). In fact, the 2009 Pew Forum survey finds that religious and mystical experiences are more common today among those who are unaffiliated with any particular religion (30%) than they were in the 1960s among the public as a whole (22%).

—Pew Research Center (2009)

Attachment is the great fabricator of illusions; reality
can be attained only by someone who is detached.

—Simone Weil

We need to take dreams more literally, and waking life
more symbolically.

—Robert Moss

Paranoia is having all the facts.

——Edmund White, paraphrasing and summarizing
William S. Burroughs

Our conscious motivations, ideas, and beliefs are a blend of false information, biases, irrational passions, rationalizations, prejudices, in which morsels of truth swim around and give the reassurance, albeit false, that the whole mixture is real and true. The thinking process attempts to organize this whole cesspool of illusions according to the laws of logic and plausibility. This level of consciousness is supposed to reflect reality; it is the map we use for organizing our life.

—Erich Fromm

What was once called the objective world is a sort of Rorschach ink blot, into which each culture, each type of personality, reads a meaning only remotely derived from the shape and color of the blot itself.

—Lewis Mumford

Fact explains nothing. On the contrary, it is fact that requires explanation.

—Marilynne Robinson

Reality is not always probable, or likely.

—Jorge Luis Borges

Of course, sometimes it's quite difficult to know if you're hallucinating. You might hallucinate a silver pen on your desk right now and never suspect it's not real—because its presence is plausible. It's easy to spot a hallucination only when it's bizarre. For all we know, we hallucinate all the time.

—David Eagleman

Questions confine answers. When there are no longer questions, answers are no longer bound by them.

—Lao Tzu (adapted by Ray Grigg)

The days of thinking of time as a river—evenly flowing, always advancing—are over. Time perception, just like vision, is a construction of the brain and is shockingly easy to manipulate experimentally.

—David Eagleman

A person has all sorts of lags built into him. . . . One, the most basic, is the sensory lag, the lag between the time your senses receive something and you are able to react. . . . We are always acting on what just finished happening. It happened at least one-thirtieth of a second ago. We think we're in the present, but we aren't. The present we know is only a movie of what happened in the past.

—Tom Wolfe, paraphrasing Ken Kesey

The difference between a gun and a tree is a difference of tempo. The tree explodes every spring.

—Ezra Pound

Every act of perception is to some
degree an act of creation, and every
act of memory is to some degree
an act of imagination.

—Gerard M. Edelman

Memory is a complicated thing, a relative to truth, but not
its twin.

—Barbara Kingsolver

We tend to think of memories as monuments we once
forged and may find intact beneath the weedy growth
of years. But, in a real sense, memories are tied to and
describe the present. Formed in an idiosyncratic way when
they happened, they're also true to the moment of recall,
including how you feel, all you've experienced, and new
values, passions, and vulnerability. One never steps into the
same stream of consciousness twice.

—Diane Ackerman

When we try to pick out anything by itself, we find it hitched to everything else in the universe.

—John Muir

All our previous positions are now exposed as absurd. But people don't draw the obvious conclusion: it must also mean then that our present situation is absurd.

—Terence McKenna

There is another world, but it is in this one.

—Paul Éluard

All our separate fictions add up to joint reality.

—Stanislaw Lec

Everything you've learned in school as obvious becomes less and less obvious as you begin to study the universe. For example, there are no solids in the universe. There's not even a suggestion of a solid. There are no absolute continuums. There are no surfaces. There are no straight lines.

—R. Buckminster Fuller

Everything we call real is made of things that cannot be regarded as real.

— John Gribbin, summarizing Niels Bohr

Once upon a time, I, Chuang Chou, dreamt I was a butterfly, fluttering hither and thither, to all intents and purposes a butterfly. I was conscious only of my happiness as a butterfly, unaware that I was Chou. Soon I awaked, and there I was, veritably myself again. Now I do not know whether I was then a man dreaming I was a butterfly, or whether I am now a butterfly, dreaming I am a man.

—Chuang Chou

Beware the stories you read or tell: subtly, at night, beneath the waters of consciousness,

they are altering your world.

—Ben Okri

The media landscape of the present day is a map in search of a territory.

—J. G. Ballard

A huge percentage of the stuff that I tend to be automatically certain of is, it turns out, totally wrong and deluded.

—David Foster Wallace

A physicist is an atom's way of knowing about atoms.

—George Wald

Einstein's space is no closer to reality than Van Gogh's sky. The glory of science is not in a truth more absolute than the truth of Bach or Tolstoy, but in the act of creation itself. The scientist's discoveries impose his own order on chaos, as the composer or painter imposes his; an order that always refers to limited aspects of reality, and is based on the observer's frame of reference, which differs from period to period as a Rembrandt nude differs from a nude by Manet.

—Arthur Koestler

I think that only daring speculation can lead us further and not accumulation of facts.

—Albert Einstein

Orthodoxy can be as stubborn in science as in religion. I do not know how to shake it except by vigorous imagination that inspires unconventional work and contains within itself an elevated potential for inspired error. As the great Italian economist Vilfredo Pareto wrote: "Give me a fruitful error any time, full of seeds, bursting with its own corrections. You can keep your sterile truth for yourself." Not to mention a man named Thomas Henry Huxley who, when not in the throes of grief or the wars of parson hunting, argued that "irrationally held truths may be more harmful than reasoned errors."

—Stephen Jay Gould

The supernatural is the natural not yet understood.

—Elbert Hubbard

When you sit in a chair, you are not actually sitting there, but levitating above it at a height of one angstrom (a hundred millionth of a centimeter), your electrons and its electrons implacably opposed to any closer intimacy.

—Bill Bryson

Briefly, you can only find truth with logic if you have already found truth without it.

—G. K. Chesterton

Things are symbols of themselves.

—Chögyam Trungpa Rinpoche

I can't understand why people are frightened of new ideas. I'm frightened of the old ones.

—John Cage

There's no reality except the one contained within us. That's why so many people live an unreal life. They take images outside them for reality and never allow the world within them to assert itself.

—Hermann Hesse

You do not need to leave your room. Remain sitting at your table and listen. Do not even listen, simply wait; be quiet, still, and solitary. The world will freely offer itself to you to be unmasked. It has no choice; it will roll in ecstasy at your feet.

—Franz Kafka

Don't believe everything you think.

—Byron Katie

It is the customary fate of new truths to begin as heresies and end as superstitions.

—T. H. Huxley

Believe those who are seeking the truth.
Doubt those who find it.

—André Gide

Why abandon a belief
Merely because it ceases to be true.
Cling to it long enough, and not a doubt
It will turn true again, for so it goes.
Most of the change we think we see in life
Is due to truths being in and out of favour.

> —Robert Frost

You shall know the truth, and the truth shall
make you mad.

> —Aldous Huxley

Your brain, after all, is encased in darkness and silence in the vault of the skull. Its only contact with the outside world is via the electrical signals exiting and entering along the super-highways of nerve bundles. Because different types of sensory information (hearing, seeing, touch, and so on) are processed at different speeds by different neural architectures, your brain faces an enormous challenge: what is the best story that can be constructed about the outside world?

—David Eagleman

Our brains permit us to use such a wee fraction of their resources that, in a sense, everything we experience is a reduction. We employ drugs, yoga techniques and poetics—and a thousand more clumsy methods—in an effort just to bring things back up to normal.

—Tom Robbins

It's in our biology to trust what we see with our eyes. This makes living in a carefully

edited,

overproduced,

and Photoshopped

world very dangerous.

—Brené Brown

According to the psychologist Robert Feldman, who has spent more than four decades studying the phenomenon, we lie, on average, three times during a routine ten-minute conversation with a stranger or casual acquaintance.

—Maria Konnikova

Tell the truth and run.

Yugoslavian proverb

All generalizations are false, including this one.

—Alexander Chase

The truth knocks on the door and you say, "Go away,
I'm looking for the truth," and so it goes away. Puzzling.

—Robert M. Pirsig

You must accept the truth from whatever source it
comes.

—Maimonides

I really believe in history, and that's something people don't believe in anymore. I know that what we do and think is a historical creation. I have very few beliefs, but this is certainly a real belief: that most everything we think of as natural is historical and has roots— specifically in the late eighteenth and early nineteenth centuries, the so-called Romantic revolutionary period— and we're essentially still dealing with expectations and feelings that were formulated at that time, like ideas about happiness, individuality, radical social change, and pleasure. We were given a vocabulary that came into existence at a particular historical moment.

—Susan Sontag

I never can feel certain of any truth but from a clear perception of its beauty.

—John Keats

Facts do not exist, only interpretations.

—Friedrich Nietzsche

Humor is what happens when we're told the truth quicker and more directly than we're used to.

—George Saunders

Tell all the Truth but tell it slant—

—Emily Dickinson

The truth does not change according to our ability to stomach it.

—Flannery O'Connor

How many ideas have there been in the history of the human race that were unthinkable ten years before they appeared?

—Fyodor Dostoevsky

Man is least himself when he talks in his own person. Give him a mask, and he will tell you the truth.

—Oscar Wilde

Truth is a pathless land.

—J. Krishnamurti

LIVING

WELCOME TO THE LONGEST, SQUISHIEST section of this book, devoted to life. From day-to-day living to the cradle-to-grave arc of our lives, from poetic statements about significance to brass-tacks pieces of advice, from ways of viewing life to survival strategies, these quotes look at how to live in the immediate now, how to live until you go to bed tonight, and how to live until you die. I believe life has inherent meaning—and if not, each individual can imbue it with meaning—but in any case, at the very least these tidbits give us great pointers for having a good time and helping others make it through. Scattered throughout are clusters about happiness, anger, work, aging, death, carpe diem, failure, and experience. (Two of the most important parts of life—love and sex— get their own section, coming up next.)

When I look back on my past and think how much time I wasted on nothing, how much time has been lost in futilities, errors, laziness, incapacity to live; how little I appreciated it, how many times I sinned against my heart and soul—then my heart bleeds. Life is a gift, life is happiness, every minute can be an eternity of happiness!

—Fyodor Dostoevsky, who wrote this hours after nearly being executed by a firing squad

The price of anything is the amount of life you exchange for it.

—Henry David Thoreau

Life is made up of a series of judgments on insufficient data, and if we waited to run down all our doubts, it would flow past us.

—Learned Hand

Every day of our lives we are on the verge of making those changes that would make all the difference.

—Mignon McLaughlin

Everything in life is just for a while.

—Philip K. Dick

We are what we pretend to be, so we must be careful what we pretend to be.

—Kurt Vonnegut

If we have our own *why* of life, we shall get along with almost any *how*.

—Friedrich Nietzsche

The most decisive actions of our life—I mean those that are most likely to decide the whole course of our future—are, more often than not, unconsidered.

—André Gide

All is pattern, all life, but we can't always see the pattern when we're part of it.

—Belva Plain

Dare to be naïve.

—R. Buckminster Fuller

I want to make a poem of my life.

—Yukio Mishima

Many people today believe that cynicism requires courage. Actually, cynicism is the height of cowardice. It is innocence and open-heartedness that requires the true courage—however often we are hurt as a result of it.

—Erica Jong

Sell your cleverness and buy bewilderment.

—Rumi

The aim of life is to live, and to live means to be aware, joyously, drunkenly, serenely, divinely aware.

—Henry Miller

The great art of life is sensation; to feel that we exist, even in pain.

—Lord Byron

Remember, remember, this is now, and now, and now. Live it, feel it, cling to it. I want to become acutely aware of all I've taken for granted.

—Sylvia Plath

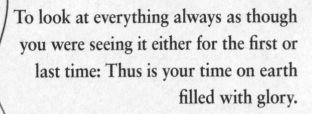

To look at everything always as though
you were seeing it either for the first or
last time: Thus is your time on earth
filled with glory.

—Betty Smith

wanderer, there is no path,
the path is made by walking.

—Antonio Machado

Do one thing every day that scares you.

—Eleanor Roosevelt

If you don't become the ocean
you'll be seasick every day.

—Leonard Cohen

All of our miseries are nothing but attachment.

—Osho

I should be suspicious of what I want.

—Rumi

A good traveler has no fixed plans and is not intent on arriving.

—Lao Tzu

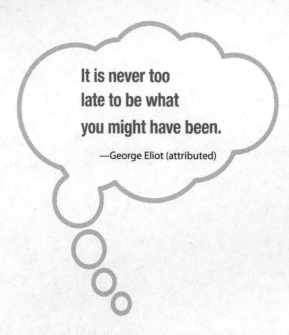

**It is never too
late to be what
you might have been.**

—George Eliot (attributed)

Life is something that happens to you while you're
making other plans.

—Margaret Millar

Your task is not to foresee the future, but to enable it.

—Antoine de Saint-Exupéry

My life is my message.

—Mohandas Gandhi

The best way out is always through.

—Robert Frost

To know what is right and not to do it is the worst
cowardice.

—Confucius

Study nothing except in the knowledge that you already knew it. Worship nothing except in adoration of your true self. And fear nothing except in the certainty that you are your enemy's begetter and its only hope of healing.

—Clive Barker

Do not seek to follow in the footsteps of the men of old; seek what they sought.

—Matsuo Bashō

It is human nature to think wisely and act in an absurd fashion.

—Anatole France

The problem is not to find the answer;
it's to face the answer.

—Terence McKenna

**All our final decisions are made
in a state of mind that is
not going to last.**

—Marcel Proust

It's easier to ask forgiveness than it is to get permission.

—Grace Hopper

The road of excess leads to the palace of wisdom.

—William Blake

I think I don't regret a single excess of my responsive youth—I only regret, in my chilled age, certain occasions and possibilities I didn't embrace.

—Henry James

Many an attack of depression is nothing but the expression of regret at having to be virtuous.

—Wilhelm Stekel

My candle burns at both ends;
  It will not last the night;
But ah, my foes, and oh, my friends—
  It gives a lovely light!

—Edna St. Vincent Millay

You will do **foolish things**, but do them with **enthusiasm.**

—Colette

Maybe all one can do is hope to end up with the right regrets.

—Arthur Miller

My great religion is a belief in the blood, the flesh, as being wiser than the intellect. We can go wrong in our minds. But what our blood feels and believes and says, is always true. The intellect is only a bit and a bridle. What do I care about knowledge? All I want is to answer to my blood, direct, without fribbling intervention of mind, or moral, or what-not.

—D. H. Lawrence

Don't postpone joy until you've learned all your lessons. Joy is your lesson.

—Alan Cohen

About morals, I know only that what is moral is what you feel good after and what is immoral is what you feel bad after.

—Ernest Hemingway

My father warned me about men and booze, but he never mentioned a word about women and cocaine.

—Tallulah Bankhead

You never know what is enough unless you know what is more than enough.

—William Blake

I have always lived violently, drunk hugely, eaten too much or not at all, slept around the clock or missed two nights of sleeping, worked too hard and too long in glory, or slobbed for a time in utter laziness. I've lifted, pulled, chopped, climbed, made love with joy and taken my hangovers as a consequence, not as a punishment.

—John Steinbeck

The grave's a fine and private place,
But none, I think, do there embrace.

—Andrew Marvell

Between two evils, I generally like to pick the one I never tried before.

—Mae West

There is no man, however wise, who has not at some period of his youth said things, or lived in a way the consciousness of which is so unpleasant to him in later life that he would gladly, if he could, expunge it from his memory.

—Marcel Proust

Saintliness is also a temptation.

—Jean Anouilh

The act of defending any of the cardinal virtues has today all the exhilaration of a vice.

—G. K. Chesterton

For how can I be sure
I shall see again
The world on the first of May
Shining after the rain?

—Jerry Gillies

Because we don't know when we will die, we get to
think of life as an inexhaustible well. Yet everything
happens only a certain number of times, and a very
small number really. . . . How many more times will you
watch the full moon rise? Perhaps twenty. And yet it all
seems limitless.

—Paul Bowles

Each

small task

of everyday life is part of the

total harmony

of the universe.

—Saint Thérèse de Lisieux

There are two ways to wash the dishes.
The first is to wash the dishes
in order to have clean dishes,
and the second is to wash the dishes
in order to wash the dishes.

—Thich Nhat Hanh

Your daily life is your temple and your religion.

—Kahlil Gibran

Before enlightenment: chop wood, carry water. After enlightenment: chop wood, carry water.

—Zen Buddhist saying

Remember that not getting what you want is sometimes a wonderful stroke of luck.

—Tenzin Gyatso, Fourteenth Dalai Lama

You never know what worse luck your bad luck has saved you from.

—Cormac McCarthy

Don't fear failure.

Not failure, but low aim, is the crime.
In great attempts

it is glorious even to fail.

—Bruce Lee

I love my rejection slips. They show me I try.

—Sylvia Plath

You miss 100% of the shots you never take.

—Wayne Gretzky

The person who says it cannot be done should not interrupt the person who is doing it.

—Chinese proverb

I have not failed. I've just found 10,000 ways that won't work.

—Thomas Edison (attributed)

When we can begin to take our failures nonseriously, it means we are ceasing to be afraid of them. It is of immense importance to learn to laugh at ourselves.

—Katherine Mansfield

Where you stumble and fall, there you discover the gold.

—Joseph Campbell

Work begins when the fear of doing nothing at all finally trumps the terror of doing it badly.

—Alain de Botton

 Try again. Fail again. Fail better.

—Samuel Beckett

Fall seven times; stand up eight.

—Japanese proverb

One doesn't discover new lands without consenting to lose sight, for a very long time, of the shore.

—André Gide

I'm glad to be here. I'm glad to be anywhere.

—Keith Richards

*You will recognize your own
path when you come upon it
because you will suddenly
have all the energy and
imagination you
will ever need.*

—Sara Teasdale

I hope for nothing. I fear nothing. I am free.

—Nikos Kazantzakis

I do not know which to prefer,
The beauty of inflections
Or the beauty of innuendoes,
The blackbird whistling
Or just after.

—Wallace Stevens

Good judgment comes from **experience.**

Experience

comes from bad judgment.

—Jim Horning

Personally I'm always ready to learn, although I do not always like being taught.

—Winston Churchill

Experience is a hard teacher because she gives the test first, the lesson after.

—Vernon Law

There are some things you learn best in calm, and some in storm.

—Willa Cather

You live out the confusions until they become clear.

—Anaïs Nin

Nothing is a waste of time if you use the experience wisely.

—Auguste Rodin

The future is made of the same stuff as the present.

—Simone Weil

Nothing in life is to be feared. It is only to be understood.

—Marie Curie

The thing that I have learned is that vulnerability is at the center of fear and shame, but it is also at the center of joy and gratitude and love and belonging.

—Brené Brown

It is so easy to be solemn; it is so hard to be frivolous.

—G. K. Chesterton

Much unhappiness has come
into the world because
of bewilderment and
things left unsaid.

—Fyodor Dostoevsky

Each time we don't say what we want to say,
we're dying.

—Yoko Ono

I would rather be ashes than dust! I would rather that my spark should burn out in a brilliant blaze than it should be stifled by dry-rot. I would rather be a superb meteor, every atom of me in magnificent glow, than a sleepy and permanent planet. The function of man is to live, not to exist. I shall not waste my days trying to prolong them. I shall use my time.

—Jack London

I have a very simple creed: that life and joy and beauty are better than dusty death.

—Bertrand Russell

Life shrinks or expands in proportion to one's courage.

—Anaïs Nin

**Let life happen to you. Believe me:
life is in the right, always.**

—Rainer Maria Rilke

I'm no longer quite sure what the question is, but I do know that the answer is "Yes."

—Leonard Bernstein

There are only two mantras:
yum and yuck. Mine is yum.

—Tom Robbins

I dwell in possibility.

—Emily Dickinson

The cave you fear to enter contains
the treasure you seek.

—Joseph Campbell (paraphrased)

You often meet your fate
on the road you take to avoid it.

—French proverb

Nature loves courage. . . . You make the commitment, and nature will respond to that commitment by removing impossible obstacles. Dream the impossible dream, and the world will not grind you under; it will lift you up. This is the trick. This is what all these teachers and philosophers who really counted, who really touched the alchemical gold, this is what they understood. This is the shamanic dance in the waterfall. This is how magic is done. It's done by hurling yourself into the abyss and discovering that it's a feather bed.

—Terence McKenna

I attribute my success to this: I never gave or took any excuse.

—Florence Nightingale

I don't like work—no man does—but I like what is in
the work—the chance to find yourself.

—Joseph Conrad

To live is so startling, it leaves but little room for other
occupations.

—Emily Dickinson

Build your own dreams, or someone else will hire you to
build theirs.

—Farrah Gray

There is as much dignity
in tilling a field as in
writing a poem.

—Booker T. Washington

Everything considered, work is less boring than amusing
oneself.

—Charles Baudelaire

The price one pays for pursuing any profession or calling is an intimate knowledge of its ugly side.

—James Baldwin

Get fired. If you're not pushing hard enough to get fired, you're not pushing hard enough.

—Tom Peters

What looks like laziness is often exhaustion.

—Chip Heath and Dan Heath

Another belief of mine: that everyone else my age is an adult, whereas I am merely in disguise.

—Margaret Atwood

We don't understand life any better at forty than at twenty, but by then we realize it and admit it.

—Jules Renard

Having devoted the first half of my life to the dark, I feel obliged to revere any pinpoint of light now.

—Mary Karr

You show me anyone who's lived to over seventy, and you show me a fighter—someone who's got the will to live.

—Agatha Christie

Here is the test to find whether your mission on Earth is finished: if you're alive, it isn't.

—Richard Bach

Don't be afraid of death so much as an inadequate life.

—Bertolt Brecht

It is sad to grow old but nice to ripen.

—Brigitte Bardot

Old age has its pleasures, which, though different, are not less than the pleasures of youth.

—W. Somerset Maugham

I used to think getting old was about vanity—but actually it's about losing people you love. Getting wrinkles is trivial.

—Joyce Carol Oates

There is only one way to be prepared for death: to be sated. In the soul, in the heart, in the spirit, in the flesh. To the brim.

—Henry de Montherlant

People living deeply have no fear of death.

—Anaïs Nin

To die will be an awfully big adventure.

—Peter Pan (J. M. Barrrie)

We are born in simplicity but die of complications.

—Pete Seeger

In spite of illness, in spite even of the archenemy sorrow, one can remain alive long past the usual date of disintegration if one is unafraid of change, insatiable in intellectual curiosity, interested in big things, and happy in small ways.

—Edith Wharton

The only thing I regret about my past is the length of it. If I had to live my life again, I'd make the same mistakes, only sooner.

—Tallulah Bankhead

Death is something we shouldn't fear because, while we are, death isn't, and when death is, we aren't.

—Antonio Machado

Death is not the opposite of life, but a part of it.

—Haruki Murakami

The call of death is a call of love. Death can be sweet if we answer it in the affirmative, if we accept it as one of the great eternal forms of life and transformation.

—Hermann Hesse

If life must not be taken too seriously—then so neither must death.

—Samuel Butler

Obituaries are like near-death experiences for cowards. Reading them is a way for me to think about death while also keeping it at arm's length. Obituaries aren't really about death; they're about life. . . . Reading about people who are dead now and did things with their lives makes me want to get up and do something decent with mine. Thinking about death every morning makes me want to live.

—Austin Kleon

I had a lover's quarrel with the world.

—Robert Frost's epitaph

There is a determined though unseen bravery, which defends itself foot to foot in the darkness against the fatal invasions of necessity and dishonesty. Noble and mysterious triumphs which no eye sees, which no renown rewards, which no flourish of triumph salutes. Life, misfortunes, isolation, abandonment, poverty, are battle-fields which have their heroes; obscure heroes, sometimes greater than the illustrious heroes.

—Victor Hugo

You can do anything in this world if you are prepared to take the consequences.

—W. Somerset Maugham

Trust only movement. Life happens at the level of events not of words. Trust movement.

—Alfred Adler

The unhappy person resents it when you try to cheer him up, because that means he has to stop dwelling on himself and start paying attention to the universe. Unhappiness is the ultimate form of self-indulgence.

—Tom Robbins

A multitude of small delights constitutes happiness.

—Charles Baudelaire

You will never be happy if you continue to search for what happiness consists of. You will never live if you are looking for the meaning of life.

—Albert Camus

People say that what we're all seeking is a meaning
for life. I don't think that's what we're really seeking. I
think what we're seeking is an experience of being alive,
so that our life experiences on the purely physical plane
will have resonance within our own innermost being
and reality, so that we actually feel the rapture of being
alive. That's what it's all finally about.

—Joseph Campbell

Be happy. It's one way of being wise.

—Colette

For all that has been—**thanks**.
For all that will be—**yes**.

—Dag Hammarskjöld

Seek not happiness too greedily, and be not fearful of unhappiness.

—Lao Tzu

Man is unhappy because he doesn't know he's happy. It's only that.

—Fyodor Dostoevsky

Truth is not always the best basis for happiness. There are certain lies which may constitute a far better and more secure foundation of happiness. There are people who perish when their eyes are opened.

—Wilhelm Stekel

If only we'd stop trying to be happy we'd have a pretty good time.

—Edith Wharton

I cannot believe the purpose of life is to be happy.
I think the purpose of life is to be useful, to be responsible, to be compassionate. It is, above all, to matter, to count, to stand for something, to have made some difference that you lived at all.

—Leo Rosten

One of the keys to happiness is a bad memory.

—Rita Mae Brown (attributed)

Happiness
is when what you think, what
you say, and what you do are in
harmony.

—Mohandas Gandhi

There are short-cuts to happiness, and dancing is
one of them.

—Vicki Baum

Although the world is very full of suffering, it is also full
of the overcoming of it.

—Helen Keller

To live is an aggression. You're involved with aggressions on all levels when you move around the world, you're occupying a space that other people can't occupy, you're stepping on flora, fauna, and little creatures as you walk. So there is a normal aggression that is part of the rhythm of living.

—Susan Sontag

There are only two or three human stories, and they go on repeating themselves as fiercely as if they had never happened before.

—Willa Cather

You live your life as if it's real.

—Leonard Cohen

Only the ideas that we actually live are of any value.

—Hermann Hesse

Waste no more time arguing about what a good person should be. Be one.

—Marcus Aurelius

If you wish to live, you must first attend your own funeral.

—Katherine Mansfield

Who will tell whether one happy moment of love or the joy of breathing or walking on a bright morning and smelling the fresh air, is not worth all the suffering and effort which life implies.

—Erich Fromm

There is nothing to find, only to realize. There is nothing to become, only to be. There is nothing to fear, only to love.

—Marianne Williamson

Heaven is home. Utopia is here. Nirvana is now.

—Edward Abbey

Believe in the holy contour of life.

—Jack Kerouac

Evil is boring. Cynicism is pointless. Fear is a bad habit. Despair is lazy. Hopelessness is self-indulgent. On the other hand: Joy is fascinating. Love is an act of heroic genius. Pleasure is our birthright. Chronic ecstasy is a learnable skill.

—Rob Brezsny

What a wonderful life I've had! I only wish I'd realized it sooner.

—Colette

LOVE

As a hopeless romantic, I've always been drawn to quotes about love, especially those that sing its praises and acknowledge its untamable power, its glory. But as a hapless romantic, who's had his heart sliced and diced and handed to him many times—and, regrettably, perhaps unavoidably, has done the same to others—I also value the quotes that look at the nitty-gritty of love—its harsh realities, but also its nuances, apparent contradictions, and unknowability. A number of the people here point out that a romantic, loving relationship, though it may start explosively and without warning, won't continue without hard work and sacrifice. A cluster a little over halfway through looks specifically at marriage. No snide comments about husbands or wives here, only thoughtful, hard-core observations about what can make a commitment last a lifetime. Speaking of hard-core, a set about sex comes next. As with love, some of these quotes revel in the power and beauty of the activity, while others offer grounded observations. A few poets coo in our ear, and we get opposing viewpoints on whether or not sex is dirty. (Either way, everyone is a fan.) Closing us out is a suite of gorgeous thoughts about a different kind of love—an all-embracing love of humanity, of all people.

For one human being to love another human being: that is perhaps the most difficult task that has been entrusted to us, the ultimate task, the final test and proof, the work for which all other work is merely preparation.

—Rainer Maria Rilke

I am the least difficult of men. All I want is boundless love.

—Frank O'Hara

I don't want to live—I want to love first and live incidentally.

—Zelda Fitzgerald, to F. Scott Fitzgerald

A kind of light spread out from her. And everything changed color. And the world opened out. And a day was good to awaken to. And there were no limits to anything. And the people of the world were good and handsome. And I was not afraid any more.

—John Steinbeck

Not the artful postures of love, but love that overthrows life. Unbiddable, ungovernable, like a riot in the heart, and nothing to be done, come ruin or rapture.

—*Shakespeare in Love* (writers Marc Norman and Tom Stoppard)

Half—the most beautiful half—of life is hidden from him who has not loved passionately.

—Stendhal

One hour of right-down love is worth an age of dully living on.

—Aphra Behn

Measured with magnetic field meters, the electromagnetic field that the heart produces is some 5,000 times more powerful than that created by the brain.

—Stephen Harrod Buhner

Do you want me to tell you something really subversive?
Love is everything it's cracked up to be. . . . It really is
worth fighting for, being brave for, risking everything
for. And the trouble is, if you don't risk anything, you
risk even more.

—Erica Jong

Of all forms of caution, caution in love is perhaps the
most fatal to true happiness.

—Bertrand Russell

Love is the flower of life, and blossoms unexpectedly
and without law, and must be plucked where it is found,
and enjoyed for the brief hour of its duration.

—D. H. Lawrence

Perhaps the feelings that we experience when we are in love represent a normal state. Being in love shows a person who he should be.

—Anton Chekhov

We always deceive ourselves twice about the people we love—first to their advantage, then to their disadvantage.

—Albert Camus

The hardest-learned lesson: that people have only their kind of love to give, not our kind.

—Mignon McLaughlin

We waste time looking for the perfect lover instead of creating the perfect love.

—Tom Robbins

The Eskimo has fifty-two names for snow because it is important to them; there ought to be as many for love.

—Margaret Atwood

Love requires the utmost vulnerability. We equip someone with freshly sharpened knives; strip naked; then invite him to stand close. What could be scarier?

—Diane Ackerman

If two people love each other there can be no happy end to it.

—Ernest Hemingway

Love doesn't just sit there, like a stone, it has to be made, like bread; remade all the time, made new.

—Ursula K. Le Guin

I have fallen in love
with someone who is hiding
inside of you.

—Hafiz

The greatest happiness love can offer is the first pressure
of hands between you and your beloved.

—Stendhal

If we are a metaphor of the universe, the human couple
is the metaphor par excellence, the point of intersection
of all forces and the seed of all forms. The couple is time
recaptured, the return to the time before time.

—Octavio Paz

Kisses are a better fate than wisdom.

—E. E. Cummings

Is suffering so very serious? I have come to doubt it. It may be quite childish, a sort of undignified pastime—I'm referring to the kind of suffering a man inflicts on a woman or a woman on a man. It's extremely painful. I agree that it's hardly bearable. But I very much fear that this sort of pain deserves no consideration at all. It's no more worthy of respect than old age or illness.

—Colette

One is never wounded by the love one gives; only by the love one expects.

—Marty Rubin

The heart has its reasons which reason
knows nothing of.

—Blaise Pascal

When so many are lonely as seem to be
lonely, it would be inexcusably selfish
to be lonely alone.

—Tennessee Williams

Loving someone is a loss of freedom—but one doesn't
think of it as loss because one gains so much else.

—Erica Jong

Love sought is good, but given unsought is better.

—William Shakespeare

Suffering for love is how I have learned practically everything I know, love of grandmother up and on.

—Djuna Barnes

I say, I believe, that one must love with all of one's being, or else live, come what may, a life of complete chastity.

—George Sand

Your task is not to seek for love,
but merely to seek and **find all of the
barriers within** yourself
that you have built against it.

—Helen Schueman

Love is the ultimate outlaw. It just won't adhere to any
rules. The most any of us can do is to sign on as its
accomplice.

—Tom Robbins

He was still too young to know that the heart's memory
eliminates the bad and magnifies the good, and that
thanks to this artifice we manage to endure the burden
of the past.

—Gabriel García Márquez

Let no one who loves be called altogether unhappy.
Even love unreturned has its rainbow.

—J. M. Barrie

The best cure for unrequited love: get to know them better.

—Alain de Botton

The heart of another is a dark forest, always, no matter how close it has been to one's own.

—Willa Cather

We are not the same persons this year as last; nor are those we love. It is a happy chance if we, changing, continue to love a changed person.

—W. Somerset Maugham

Perfect love means to love the one through whom one became unhappy.

—Søren Kierkegaard

You learn to speak by speaking, to study by studying,
to run by running, to work by working; in just the same
way, you learn to love by loving.

> — Saint Francis de Sales

Being with you and not being with you is the only way I
have to measure time.

> —Jorge Luis Borges

**For my part, I prefer my heart
to be broken. It is so lovely,
dawn-kaleidoscopic within
the crack.**

> —D. H. Lawrence

Marriage is a public declaration of
a man and a woman that they have
formed a secret alliance, with the
intention to belong to, and share with
each other, a mystical estate; mystical
exactly in the sense that the real
experience cannot be communicated to
others, nor explained even to oneself
on rational grounds.

—Katherine Anne Porter

A person's character is but half formed till after wedlock.

—Charles Simmons

Only choose in marriage a woman whom you would choose as a friend if she were a man.

—Joseph Joubert

Never marry a man who hates his mother because he'll end up hating you.

—Jill Bennett

In every marriage more than a week old, there are grounds for divorce. The trick is to find, and continue to find, grounds for marriage.

—Robert Anderson

One advantage of marriage is that, when you fall out of love with him or he falls out of love with you, it keeps you together until you fall in again.

—Judith Viorst

You don't marry one person; you marry three: the person you think they are, the person they are, and the person they are going to become as the result of being married to you.

—Richard Needham

Marriage isn't a love affair. It isn't even a honeymoon. It's a job. A long hard job, at which both partners have to work, harder than they've worked at anything in their lives before.

—Rosamunde Pilcher

Wasn't marriage, like life, unstimulating and unprofitable and somewhat empty when too well ordered and protected and guarded? Wasn't it finer, more splendid, more nourishing, when it was, like life itself, a mixture of the sordid and the magnificent; of mud and stars; of earth and flowers; of love and hate and laughter and tears and ugliness and beauty and hurt?

—Edna Ferber

A happy marriage is the union of two forgivers.

—Ruth Bell Graham

Many married couples separate because they quarrel incessantly, but just as many separate because they were never honest enough or courageous enough to quarrel when they should have.

—Sydney J. Harris

If you made a list of reasons why any couple got married, and another list of the reasons for their divorce, you'd have a hell of a lot of overlapping.

—Mignon McLaughlin

Love is the answer, but while you're waiting for the answer, **sex raises some pretty good questions.**

—Woody Allen

How idiotic civilization is! Why be given a body if you have to keep it shut up in a case like a rare, rare fiddle?

—Katherine Mansfield

I like my body when it is with your body.

——E. E. Cummings

All parts of the body are erotogenic.

—Leonard Cohen

The pleasure of living and the pleasure of the orgasm
are identical.

—Wilhelm Reich

Only the human mind invents categories and tries to
force facts into separated pigeon-holes. The living world
is a continuum in each and every one of its aspects. The
sooner we learn this concerning human sexual behavior,
the sooner we shall reach a sound understanding of the
realities of sex.

—Alfred Kinsey

Sex *is* the divine in its most available epiphany.

—Huston Smith

After all, what is a kiss? A vow made at closer range, a more precise promise, a confession that contains its own proof, a seal placed on a pact that has already been signed; it's a secret told to the mouth rather than to the ear.

—Edmond Rostand

Ah, when she moved, she moved more ways than one.

—Theodore Roethke

I want to do with you what spring does with
the cherry trees.

—Pablo Neruda

"Natural" is a very dangerous word to use about sexuality. . . . Our society's notions of normality are completely fake and meta-trendy, since they rely on the changing standards of superstition, religion, Christianity and gender bias to define themselves. Americans, in particular, exhibit very childish reactions to sexual practices that are new to them, much like little kids who are offered a vegetable they haven't seen before: "That's disgusting!" "But, darling, you haven't even tried it!" "I don't care, I hate it, I hate it!"

—Susie Bright

Is sex dirty? Only if it's done right.

—Woody Allen

Tell me the smallest things about yourself so long as they are obscene and secret and filthy.

—James Joyce, to Nora Barnacle Joyce

My own belief is that there is hardly anyone whose sexual life, if it were broadcast, would not fill the world at large with surprise and horror.

—W. Somerset Maugham

You must acknowledge deep in your heart of hearts that *people are supposed to fuck*. It is our main purpose in life, and all those other activities—playing the trumpet, vacuuming carpets, reading mystery novels, eating chocolate mousse—are just ways of passing the time until you can fuck again.

—Cynthia Heimel

Of all the sexual aberrations, chastity is the strangest.

—Anatole France

Sex is hardly ever just about sex.

—Shirley MacLaine

Love ain't nothing but sex misspelled.

—Harlan Ellison

Doing dirt on sex; it is the crime of our times, because what we need is tenderness towards the body, towards sex, we need tender-hearted fucking.

—D. H. Lawrence

Perhaps everything terrible is in its deepest being something that needs our love.

—Rainer Maria Rilke

The important thing
is not to think much,
but to love much,
and so to do what best
awakens us to love.

—Saint Teresa of Ávila

The more I think it over, the more I feel that there is nothing more truly artistic than to love people.

—Vincent van Gogh

That Love is all there is,
Is all we know of Love

—Emily Dickinson

WELL-BEING

AN OVERLAPPING COMPANION to the sections "Living" and "Self," the quotes I've put here on well-being tend to focus on physical, mental, and financial health. There are tips and thoughts on eating, drinking, crying, simplifying and slowing down, suffering, and handling money (or the lack thereof). There are some random bits of advice in the mix, as well as thoughts on advice itself.

Our bodies are apt to be our autobiographies.

—Gelett Burgess

We have so many words for states of mind, and so few words for the states of the body.

—Jeanne Moreau

The great majority of us are required to live a life of constant, systematic duplicity. Your health is bound to be affected if, day after day, you say the opposite of what you feel, if you grovel before what you dislike, and rejoice at what brings you nothing but misfortune.

—Boris Pasternak

The food you eat can be either the safest and most powerful form of medicine or the slowest form of poison.

—Ann Wigmore

What you eat today walks and talks tomorrow.

—Esther Blumenfeld

Don't eat anything your great-grandmother wouldn't recognize as food. . . . Don't eat anything with more than five ingredients, or ingredients you can't pronounce.

—Michael Pollan

I go to nature to be soothed and healed, and to have my senses put in order.

—John Burroughs

There must be quite a few things a hot bath won't cure, but I don't know many of them.

—Sylvia Plath

Here's a rule I recommend. Never practice two vices at once.

—Tallulah Bankhead

I think of going to the grave without having a psychedelic experience like going to the grave without ever having sex. It means that you never figured out what it is all about. The mystery is in the body and the way the body works itself
into nature.

—Terence McKenna

Abstinence is as easy to me as temperance would be difficult.

—Samuel Johnson

In wine, there is the truth.

The sway of alcohol over mankind is unquestionably
due to its power to stimulate the mystical faculties of
human nature, usually crushed to earth by the cold facts
and dry criticisms of the sober hour. Sobriety diminishes,
discriminates, and says no; drunkenness expands,
unites, and says yes. It is in fact the great exciter of the
Yes function in man. It brings its votary from the chill
periphery of things to the radiant core. It makes him for
the moment one with truth.

Always do sober what you said you'd do drunk. That will teach you to keep your mouth shut.

—Ernest Hemingway

I drank because I wanted to drown my sorrows, but now the damned things have learned to swim.

—Frida Kahlo

Drunkenness is temporary suicide.

—Bertrand Russell

Are you aware that rushing toward a goal is a sublimated death wish? It's no coincidence we call them "deadlines."

—Tom Robbins

One final paragraph of advice: do not burn yourselves out. Be as I am—a reluctant enthusiast . . . a part-time crusader, a half-hearted fanatic. Save the other half of yourselves and your lives for pleasure and adventure.

—Edward Abbey

Nature does not hurry, yet everything is accomplished.

—Lao Tzu

The rush and pressure of modern life are a form, perhaps the most common form, of its innate violence. To allow oneself to be carried away by a multitude of conflicting concerns, to surrender to too many demands, to commit oneself to too many projects, to want to help everyone in everything is to succumb to violence. More than that, it is cooperation in violence.

—Thomas Merton

When you have grown still on purpose while everything around you is asking for chaos, you will find the doors between every room of the interior castle thrown open, the path home to your true love unobstructed after all.

—St. Teresa of Ávila

Besides the noble art of getting things done, there is the noble art of leaving things undone. The wisdom of life consists in the elimination of non-essentials.

—Lin Yutang

Man suffers because of his craving to possess and keep forever things which are impermanent.

—Alan Watts

I make the most of all that comes and the least of all that goes.

—Sara Teasdale

You cannot overestimate the unimportance of practically everything.

—John Maxwell

Advice is what we ask for when we already know the answer but wish we didn't.

—Erica Jong

The worst men often give the best advice.

—Philip James Bailey

I am glad that I paid so little attention to good advice; had I abided by it I might have been saved from some of my most valuable mistakes.

—Edna St. Vincent Millay

Don't try to solve serious matters in the middle
of the night.

—Philip K. Dick

The best way to keep one's word is not to give it.

—Napoleon Bonaparte

Even when we say nothing our clothes are talking
noisily to everyone who sees us, telling them who we
are, where we come from, what we like to do in bed and
a dozen other intimate things.

—Alison Lurie

Talk to yourself like you would to someone you love.

—Brené Brown

Considering how dangerous everything is nothing is really very frightening.

—Gertrude Stein

I've been absolutely terrified every moment of my life, and I've never let it keep me from doing a single thing that I wanted to do.

—Georgia O'Keeffe

Tell your heart that the fear of suffering is worse than the suffering itself.

—Paulo Coelho

You cannot protect yourself from sadness without protecting yourself from happiness.

—Jonathan Safran Foer

Don't grieve. Anything you lose comes round in another form.

—Rumi

Nothing is as bleak as it seems at the time.

—unnamed woman quoted in *Financial Times*

The deeper that sorrow carves into your being, the more joy you can contain.

—Kahlil Gibran

The cure for pain is in the pain.

—Rumi

We are healed of a suffering only by experiencing it in full.

—Marcel Proust

There is a sacredness in tears. They are not the mark of weakness, but of power. They speak more eloquently than ten thousand tongues. They are the messengers of overwhelming grief, of deep contrition, and of unspeakable love.

—Washington Irving

Those who do not weep, do not see.

—Victor Hugo

What soap is for the body, tears are for the soul.

—Jewish proverb

Heaven knows we need never be ashamed of our tears, for they are rain upon the blinding dust of earth, overlying our hard hearts. I was better after I had cried, than before—more sorry, more aware of my own ingratitude, more gentle.

—Charles Dickens

Where can you scream? It's a serious question: where can you go in society and scream?

—R. D. Laing

The things you own
end up owning you.

—Chuck Palahniuk

In order to change skins, evolve into new cycles, I feel
one has to learn to discard. If one changes internally,
one should not continue to live with the same objects.
They reflect one's mind and psyche of yesterday. I throw
away what has no dynamic, living use.

—Anaïs Nin

Stop accumulating stuff, and start accumulating
experiences.

—James Wallman

Poverty is no disgrace to a man, but it is confoundedly inconvenient.

—Sydney Smith

He had heard people speak contemptuously of money: he wondered if they had ever tried to do without it.

—W. Somerset Maugham

There are two ways to be rich: One is by acquiring much, and the other is by desiring little.

—Jackie French Koller

I think that luxury has nothing to do
with money, and everything to do with beauty.

—Frances Moore Lappé

When you have only two pennies left in the world, buy
a loaf of bread with one, and a lily with the other.

—Chinese proverb

SELF

WHO ARE YOU? WHO ARE WE IN GENERAL? What is the self? What are emotions, and how should we handle them? What should we believe in, if anything? Oh yes, I know these questions sound unbearably pretentious. Yet reading some of the attempts to answer them—made by people around the world and throughout time—is enjoyable and provides plenty of perspectives and possibilities to perhaps phase into our lives.

The mind is everything. What you think, you become.

—Gautama Buddha

At the center of your being
you have the answer;
you know who you are
and you know what you want.

—Lao Tzu

The only tyrant I accept in this world is the still voice within.

—Mohandas Gandhi

Imagine awaking from a torpor having forgotten how your friends and family see you. Perhaps, unchained from everyone's expectations for how you ought to behave, you could be whoever you liked.

—Christian Jarrett

We are all our own graveyards I believe; we squat amongst the tombs of the people we were. If we're healthy, every day is a celebration, a Day of the Dead, in which we give thanks for the lives that we lived; and if we are neurotic we brood and mourn and wish that the past was still present.

—Clive Barker

Do I contradict myself?
Very well then, I contradict myself.
I am large.
I contain multitudes!

—Walt Whitman

Living things tend to change unrecognizably as they grow. Who would deduce the dragonfly from the larva, the iris from the bud, the lawyer from the infant? Flora or fauna, we are all shape-shifters and magical reinventors. Life is really a plural noun, a caravan of selves.

—Diane Ackerman

A biography is considered complete if it merely accounts for six or seven selves, whereas a person may well have as many as a thousand.

—Virginia Woolf

People can't live with change if there's not a changeless core inside them. The key to the ability to change is a changeless sense of who you are, what you are about and what you value.

—Stephen R. Covey

Between stimulus and response there is a
space.

In that space is our power to choose our
response.

In our response lies our growth and our
freedom.

—Viktor Frankl

It's not what happens to you, but how you react to it
that matters.

—Epictetus

"What I believe" is a process rather than a finality. Finalities are for gods and government, not for the human intellect.

—Emma Goldman

Our firmest convictions are apt to be the most suspect; they mark our limitations and our bounds.

—José Ortega y Gasset

I am not a thing—**a noun.** I seem to be **a verb,** an evolutionary process—**an integral function of the universe.**

—R. Buckminster Fuller

No feeling is final.

—Rainer Maria Rilke

Never apologize for showing feeling. When you do so, you apologize for the truth.

—Benjamin Disraeli

I am never upset
for the reason I think.

—Helen Schueman

There is no sight so ugly as the human face in anger.

—Louise Fitzhugh

No person is important enough to make me angry.

—Carlos Castaneda

Anger is a signal, and one worth listening to. . . . Just as physical pain tells us to take our hand off the hot stove, the pain of our anger preserves the very integrity of our self.

—Harriet Lerner

Anger must be the energy that has not yet found its right channel.

—Florida Scott-Maxwell

People in a temper often say a lot of silly, terrible things they mean.

—Penelope Gilliatt

A man is about as big as the things that make him angry.

—Winston Churchill

Anybody can become angry—that is easy; but to be angry with the right person, and to the right degree, and at the right time, and for the right purpose, and in the right way—that is not within everybody's power and is not easy.

—Aristotle

When angry, count four; when very angry, swear.

—Mark Twain

Anxiety is fear of one's self.

—Wilhelm Stekel

Worry a little bit every day, and in a lifetime you will lose a couple of years. If something is wrong, fix it if you can. But train yourself not to worry. Worry never fixes anything.

—Mary Hemingway

I've experienced many terrible things in my life, a few of which actually happened.

—unknown

I never saw a wild thing sorry for itself.
A small bird will drop frozen dead
from a bough without ever having
felt sorry for itself.

—D. H. Lawrence

Do you take pride in your hurt? Does it make you seem large and tragic? . . . Well, think about it. Maybe you're playing a part on a great stage with only yourself as audience.

—John Steinbeck

Reject your sense of injury, and the injury itself disappears.

—Marcus Aurelius

The best years of your life are the ones in which you decide your problems are your own. You do not blame them on your mother, the ecology, or the president. You realize that you control your own destiny.

—Albert Ellis

We are what we repeatedly do. Excellence, then, is not an act, but a habit.

—Will Durant, paraphrasing Aristotle

You are that which you are seeking.

—Saint Francis of Assisi

If you're honest, you sooner or later have to confront
your values. Then you're forced to separate what is right
from what is merely legal. This puts you metaphysically
on the run. America is full of metaphysical outlaws.

—Tom Robbins

Teachers open the door, but you must enter by yourself.

—Zen proverb

Would you like you
if you met you?

—Tegan and Sara

When I look for my existence, I do not look for it in myself.

—Antonio Porchia

People focus on role models; it is more effective to find anti-models—people you don't want to resemble when you grow up.

—Nassim N. Taleb

Lying to ourselves is more deeply ingrained than lying to others.

—Fyodor Dostoevsky

The "I" in me, my friend, dwells in the house of silence, and therein it shall remain for ever more, unperceived, unapproachable. I would not have thee believe in what I say nor trust in what I do—for my words are naught but thy own thoughts in sound and my deeds thy own hopes in action.

—Kahlil Gibran

To be a man is to be *responsible*: to be ashamed of miseries you did not cause; to be proud of your comrades' victories; to be aware, when setting one stone, that you are building a world.

—Antoine de Saint-Exupéry

Maturity: the confidence to have no opinions on many things.

—Alain de Botton

Maturity is reached the day we don't need to be lied to about anything.

—Frank Yerby

People seem not to see that their opinion of the world is also a confession of character.

—Ralph Waldo Emerson

A human being should be able to change a diaper, plan an invasion, butcher a hog, conn a ship, design a building, write a sonnet, balance accounts, build a wall, set a bone, comfort the dying, take orders, give orders, cooperate, act alone, solve equations, analyze a new problem, pitch manure, program a computer, cook a tasty meal, fight efficiently, die gallantly. Specialization is for insects.

—Robert Heinlein

Interviewer: So to you, faith is not a comfort?

Madeleine L'Engle: Good heavens, no. It's a challenge: I dare you to believe in God. I dare you to think [our existence] wasn't an accident.

Practically speaking, your religion is the story you tell about your life.

—Andrew Greeley

The trouble is I don't believe my unbelief.

—Graham Greene

Faith is not a belief.
Faith is what is left when your beliefs have
all been blown to hell.

—Ram Dass

There is only one religion, though there are a hundred
versions of it.

—George Bernard Shaw

Those who don't believe in magic will never find it.

—Roald Dahl

My faith is whatever makes me feel good about being alive. If your religion doesn't make you feel good to be alive, what the hell is the point of it?

—Tom Robbins

I don't believe anything, but I have many suspicions.

—Robert Anton Wilson

I daresay anything can be made holy by being sincerely worshippcd.

—Iris Murdoch

The third-rate mind is only happy when it is thinking with the majority. The second-rate mind is only happy when it is thinking with the minority. The first-rate mind is only happy when it is thinking.

—A. A. Milne

A wise man once said, Convention is like the shell to the chick, a protection till he is strong enough to break it through.

—Learned Hand

Don't laugh at a youth for his affectations; he is only trying on one face after another to find his own.

—Logan Pearsall Smith

If there is anything the nonconformist hates worse than a **conformist**, it's another **nonconformist** who doesn't conform to the prevailing standard of **nonconformity**.

—Bill Vaughan

The reasonable man adapts himself to the world: the unreasonable one persists in trying to adapt the world to himself. Therefore all progress depends on the unreasonable man.

—George Bernard Shaw

Even the best of us are at least part-time bastards.

---Mary Karr

What a strange machine man is! You fill him with bread, wine, fish, and radishes, and out comes sighs, laughter, and dreams.

—Nikos Kazantzakis

I am human; nothing human is alien to me.

—Terence

I took a deep breath and listened to the old brag of my heart. I am, I am, I am.

—Sylvia Plath

We ought to dance with rapture that we should be alive and in the flesh, and part of the living, incarnate cosmos. I am part of the sun as my eye is part of me. That I am part of the earth my feet know perfectly, and my blood is part of the sea. My soul knows that I am part of the human race, my soul is an organic part of the great human soul, as my spirit is part of my nation. In my own very self, I am part of my family. There is nothing of me that is alone and absolute except my mind, and we shall find that the mind has no existence by itself, it is only the glitter of the sun on the surface of the waters.

—D. H. Lawrence

Man is the only animal for whom his own existence is a problem which he has to solve.

—Erich Fromm

The amazing thing is that every atom in your body came from a star that exploded. And, the atoms in your left hand probably came from a different star than your right hand. It really is the most poetic thing I know about physics.

—Lawrence M. Krauss

Every atom you possess has almost certainly passed through several stars and been part of millions of organisms on its way to becoming you. We are each so atomically numerous and so vigorously recycled at death that a significant number of our atoms—up to a billion for each of us, it has been suggested—probably once belonged to Shakespeare. A billion more each came from Buddha and Genghis Khan and Beethoven, and any other historical figure you care to name.

—Bill Bryson

We are dead stars looking back up at the sky.

—Michelle Thaller

There are more molecules of water in a cup of water
than cups of water in all the world's oceans. This means
that some molecules in every cup of water you drink
passed through the kidneys of Genghis Khan, Napoleon,
Abe Lincoln or any other historical person of your
choosing. Same goes for air: There are more molecules
of air in a single breath of air than there are breaths
of air in Earth's entire atmosphere. Therefore, some
molecules of air you inhale passed through the lungs of
Billy the Kid, Joan of Arc, Beethoven, Socrates or any
other historical person of your choosing.

—Neil deGrasse Tyson

I believe in the flesh and the appetites,
Seeing, hearing, feeling, are miracles, and each part and
tag of me is a miracle.

Divine am I inside and out, and I make holy whatever I
touch or am touch'd from,
The scent of these arm-pits aroma finer than prayer,
This head more than churches, bibles, and all the creeds.

—Walt Whitman

Finally I am coming to the conclusion that my highest ambition is to be what I already am.

—Thomas Merton

You're braver than you believe, and stronger than you seem, and smarter than you think.

—A. A. Milne

OTHERS

A BUNCH OF PRETTY SMART PEOPLE throughout history think that we *are* our relationships with other people. Any person as an individual is meaningless, perhaps nonexistent is some senses. We are who we are only in combination with others: lovers, spouses, exes, blood family, in-laws, friends, enemies, neighbors, coworkers, bosses, acquaintances, your dentist, your mechanic, the cashier who rang you up at the grocery store, the guy who flipped you off at the stoplight. We're inherently as formless as water, and all of our relationships comprise the glass that gives us shape. Put another way, we're each a cell in a larger organism, and no cell can survive on its own. Taking this line of thought further, a common thread in mysticism is that there is literally no separation between people; at some level, we're all one. The appearance of a self and others is an illusion here in the *maya* (the Hindu word for this level of reality). Now, even if you don't subscribe to either of these views, they signal the extreme importance of our interactions with others. Even if you don't think that others are everything that defines us, those relationships are an enormous part of who we are. They involve a huge amount of our time, energy, and brainpower. We're almost always relating to others. Even when we're alone, we're often thinking of others—planning, plotting, fantasizing, mentally replaying conversations. . . . But how to get along with them? What's their significance, how should we treat them, and how should we handle their treatment of us?

Man is a knot, a web, a mesh into
which relationships are tied.
Only those relationships matter.

—Antoine de Saint-Exupéry

No man is an island, entire of itself; every man is a piece
of the continent, a part of the main; if a clod be washed
away by the sea, Europe is the less, as well as if a
promontory were, as well as if a manner of thy friends
or thine own were; any man's death diminishes me,
because I am involved in mankind. And therefore never
send to know for whom the bell tolls; it tolls for thee.

—John Donne

I am a part of all that I have met.

—Alfred, Lord Tennyson

Call it a clan, call it a network, call it a tribe, call it a
family: Whatever you call it, whoever you are,
you need one.

—Jane Howard

We are born for cooperation, as are the feet, the hands,
the eyelids, and the upper and lower jaws.

—Marcus Aurelius

The only people for me are the mad ones, the ones who
are mad to live, mad to talk, mad to be saved, desirous
of everything at the same time, the ones who never yawn
or say a commonplace thing, but burn, burn, burn like
fabulous yellow roman candles exploding like spiders
across the stars and in the middle you see the blue
centerlight pop and everybody goes Awww!

—Jack Kerouac

When you are in love with humanity, you are satisfied with yourself.

—Luigi Pirandello

I look upon the whole world as my fatherland, and every war has to me a horror of a family feud. I look upon true patriotism as the brotherhood of man and the service of all to all.

—Helen Keller

When young, one is confident to be able to build palaces for mankind, but when the time comes one has one's hands full just to be able to remove their trash.

—Johann Wolfgang von Goethe

If you want to

change the way

people respond to you,

change the way

you respond to people.

—Timothy Leary

Don't take anything personally. Nothing others do is because of you. What others say and do is a projection of their own reality, their own dream.

—don Miguel Ruiz

Nothing is a greater impediment to being on good terms with others than being ill at ease with yourself.

—Honoré de Balzac

The only common denominator in all your fucked-up relationships is you.

—bumper sticker

I have perceiv'd that to be with those I like is enough.

—Walt Whitman

There are days when solitude is a heady wine that intoxicates you with freedom, others when it is a bitter tonic, and still others when it is a poison that makes you beat your head against the wall.

—Colette

The meeting of two personalities is like the contact of two chemical substances. If there is any reaction, both are transformed.

—Carl Jung

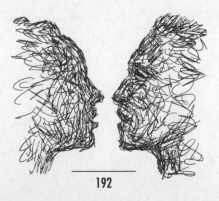

The way to learn whether a person is trustworthy is to trust him.

—Ernest Hemingway

That which the sober man keeps in his breast, the drunken man lets out at the lips. Astute people, when they want to ascertain a man's true character, make him drunk.

—Martin Luther

Do not do unto others as you would expect they should do unto you. Their tastes may not be the same.

—George Bernard Shaw

Sorry means you feel the pulse of other people's pain as well as your own, and saying it means you take a share of it. And so it binds us together, makes us trodden and sodden as one another. *Sorry* is a lot of things. It's a hole refilled. A debt repaid. *Sorry* is the wake of misdeed. It's the crippling ripple of consequence. *Sorry* is sadness, just as knowing is sadness. *Sorry* is sometimes self-pity. But *Sorry*, really, is not about you. It's theirs to take or leave.

—Craig Silvey

Never ruin an apology with an excuse.

—Benjamin Franklin

He that cannot **forgive** others
breaks the bridge over which
he must pass himself, for every man
hath need to **be forgiven.**

—Edward Herbert, First Baron Herbert of Cherbury

A stiff apology is a second insult. The injured party
does not want to be compensated because he has
been wronged; he wants to be healed because he has
been hurt.

—G. K. Chesterton

To understand completely is to forgive completely.

—French proverb (modified)

If you had never condemned, you would not need to forgive.

—Anthony de Mello

Before you embark on a journey of revenge,
dig two graves.

—Confucius

The best revenge is to be unlike him who performed
the injury.

—Marcus Aurelius

Do not free a camel of the burden of his hump; you may be freeing him from being a camel.

—G. K. Chesterton

When I walk into a room, I know that everyone in it loves me. I just don't expect them to realize it yet.

—Byron Katie

People come into your life for a reason, a season, or a lifetime. When you know which one it is, you will know what to do for that person.

—unknown

If you hate a person, you hate something in him that is part of yourself. What isn't part of ourselves doesn't disturb us.

—Hermann Hesse

Everything that irritates us about others can lead us to an understanding of ourselves.

—Carl Jung

The fault you see in your brother is really in you. The world is a mirror.

—Rumi

I permit no man to narrow and degrade my soul by making me hate him.

—Booker T. Washington

Whenever you have trouble with all [group name here], it isn't about [group name here], it's about you. I've found this to be a useful self-diagnostic tool.

—Carolyn Hax

I imagine one of the reasons
people cling to their hates so stubbornly is
because they sense, **once hate is gone,**
they will be forced to deal with pain.

—James Baldwin

When you know how to listen,
everyone is the guru.

—Ram Dass

Everyone you will ever meet knows something
you don't.

—Bill Nye, the Science Guy

When people talk, listen completely. Don't be thinking
what you're going to say. Most people never listen.

—Ernest Hemingway

Three things in human life are important. The first is to be kind. The second is to be kind. And the third is to be kind.

—Henry James

What do we live for, if it is not to make life less difficult for each other?

—George Eliot

One of the deep secrets of life is that all that is really worth doing is what we do for others.

—Lewis Carroll

If you want others to be happy, practice compassion. If you want to be happy, practice compassion.

—Tenzin Gyatso, Fourteenth Dalai Lama

What **wisdom** can you find that is greater than **kindness**?

—Jean-Jacques Rousseau

Treat the other man's faith gently; it is all he has to believe with. His mind was created for his own thoughts, not yours or mine.

—Henry S. Haskins

We are all in the same boat in a stormy sea, and we owe each other a terrible loyalty.

—G. K. Chesterton

We're all going to die, all of us, what a circus! That alone should make us love each other but it doesn't. We are terrorized and flattened by trivialities, we are eaten up by nothing.

—Charles Bukowski

A hurtful act is the transference to others of the degradation which we bear in ourselves.

—Simone Weil

The man who is
brutally honest
enjoys the brutality
quite as much as the honesty.
Possibly more.

—Richard Needham

A truth that's told with bad intent
Beats all the lies you can invent.

—William Blake

Try to say nothing negative about anybody for three days, for forty-five days, for three months. See what happens to your life.

—Yoko Ono

Everyone in life is gonna hurt you; you just have to figure out which people are worth the pain.

—Erica Baican

Never answer an angry word with an angry word. It's the second one that makes the quarrel.

—W. A. Nance

It is very unnerving to be proven wrong, particularly when you are really right and the person who is really wrong is proving you wrong and proving himself, wrongly, right.

—Lemony Snicket

The longer we live, the more we find we are like other persons.

—Oliver Wendell Holmes, Sr.

I judge people by what they might be,—not are, nor will be.

—Robert Browning

To be good we must needs have suffered; but perhaps it is necessary to have caused suffering before we can become better.

—Maurice Maeterlinck

I refuse to make a hierarchy of human actions and ascribe worthiness to some and ill-repute to others. The terms vice and virtue have no signification for me. I do not confer praise or blame: I accept.

—W. Somerset Maugham

You have enemies? Why, it is the story of every man who has done a great deed or created a new idea.

—Victor Hugo

Pay attention to your enemies, for they are the first to discover your mistakes.

—Antisthenes

If we could read the secret history of our enemies, we should find in each person's life sorrow and suffering enough to disarm all hostility.

—Henry Wadsworth Longfellow

Am I not destroying my enemies when I make friends of them?

—Abraham Lincoln

Saints choose to think of everyone as their friend, so that hate does not get in their way.

—Rumi

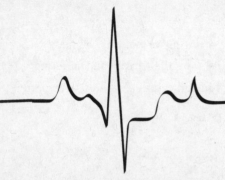

It's all very well to tell us to forgive our enemies; our enemies can never hurt us very much. But oh, what about forgiving our friends?

    —Willa Cather

As rare as true love is, true friendship is still rarer.

    —François de La Rochefoucauld

One friend in a lifetime is much; two are many; three are hardly possible.

    —Henry Brooks Adams

It's the friends that you can call up at 4 a.m. that matter.

—Marlene Dietrich

It's no good trying to keep up old friendships. It's painful for both sides. The fact is, one grows out of people, and the only thing is to face it.

—W. Somerset Maugham

The friendships which last are those wherein each friend respects the other's dignity to the point of not really wanting anything from him.

—Cyril Connolly

Friendship has splendors that love knows not.

—Mariama Bâ

214

Our perfect companions never have fewer than four feet.

—Colette

I once had a sparrow alight upon my shoulder for a
moment while I was hoeing in a village garden, and I felt
that I was more distinguished by that circumstance than
I should have been by any epaulet I could have worn.

—Henry David Thoreau

The animal shall not be measured by man. In a world older and more complete than ours, they move finished and complete, gifted with extension of the senses we have lost or never attained, living by voices we shall never hear. They are not brethren; they are not underlings; they are other nations, caught with ourselves in the net of life and time, fellow prisoners of the splendor and travail of the earth.

—Henry Beston

We never consider that the things dogs know about us are things of which we have not the faintest notion.

—José Saramago

One realizes that even in harmonious families there is this double life: the group life, which is the one we can observe in our neighbour's household, and, underneath, another—secret and passionate and intense—which is the real life that stamps the faces and gives character to the voices of our friends. Always in his mind each member of these social units is escaping, running away, trying to break the net which circumstances and his own affections have woven about him. One realizes that human relationships are the tragic necessity of human life; that they can never be wholly satisfactory, that every ego is half the time greedily seeking them, and half the time pulling away from them. In those simple relationships of loving husband and wife, affectionate sisters, children and grandmother, there are innumerable shades of sweetness and anguish which make up the pattern of our lives day by day.

—Willa Cather

He that has no fools, knaves, or beggars in his family was begot by a flash of lightning.

—English proverb

Happy or unhappy, families are all mysterious. We have only to imagine how differently we would be described—and will be, after our deaths—by each of the family members who believe they know us.

—Gloria Steinem

If you think you're enlightened, go spend a week with your family.

—Ram Dass

Sibling relationships—and 80 percent of Americans have at least one—outlast marriages, survive the death of parents, resurface after quarrels that would sink any friendship. They flourish in a thousand incarnations of closeness and distance, warmth, loyalty and distrust.

—Erica E. Goode

Nobody has ever before asked the nuclear family to live all by itself in a box the way we do. With no relatives, no support, we've put it in an impossible situation.

—Margaret Mead

When I have spoken of my family in the past, there is always someone who wants to know how such love and fury could coexist, and I don't understand the question. Families seem to me to be *made* of love and fury. The world is mostly water; we are mostly water; life itself is mostly water, but we don't ask how such hydrogen and oxygen can coexist. We just drink it and live.

—Richard Hoffman

Family life! The United Nations is child's play compared to the tugs and splits and need to understand and forgive in any family.

—May Sarton

Before I got married I had six theories about bringing up children. Now I have six children and no theories.

—John Wilmot, Earl of Rochester

We don't yet know, above all, what the world might be like if children were to grow up without being subjected to humiliation, if parents would respect them and take them seriously as people.

—Alice Miller

The more boring a child is, the more the parents, when showing off the child, receive adulation for being good parents because they have a tame child-creature in their house.

—Frank Zappa

The art of parenting: how constantly to break a lot of bad news—without destroying all confidence and hope.

—Alain de Botton

The reason grandparents and grandchildren get along so well is that they have a common enemy.

—Sam Levenson

Children begin by loving their parents; as they grow
older they judge them; sometimes they forgive them.

—Oscar Wilde

**All parents damage their children. It
cannot be helped. Youth, like pristine glass,
absorbs the prints of its handlers. Some
parents smudge, others crack, a few shatter
childhoods completely into jagged little
pieces, beyond repair.**

—Mitch Albom

If you have never been hated
by your child, you have never
been a parent.

—Bette Davis

The end product of child-raising is not the child but the parent.

—Frank Pittman

If there is anything we wish to change in the child, we should first examine it and see whether it is not something that could be better changed in ourselves.

—Carl Jung

Adults find pleasure in deceiving a child. They consider it necessary, but they also enjoy it. The children very quickly figure it out and then practice deception themselves.

—Elias Canetti

Children don't need to be taught how to learn; they are born learners. They come out of the womb interacting with and exploring their surroundings. Babies are active learners, their burning curiosity motivating them to learn how the world works. And if they are given a safe, supportive environment, they will continue to learn hungrily and naturally—in the manner and at the speed that suits them best.

—Wendy Priesnitz

There is probably no more terrible instance of enlightenment than the one in which you discover your father is a man—with human flesh.

—Frank Herbert

The fundamental defect of fathers is that they want their children to be a credit to them.

—Bertrand Russell

It doesn't matter who my father was; it matters who I remember he was.

—Anne Sexton

The mother-child relationship is paradoxical and, in a sense, tragic. It requires the most intense love on the mother's side, yet this very love must help the child grow away from the mother, and to become fully independent.

—Erich Fromm

A mother never realizes that her children are no longer children.

—Holbrook Jackson

Other things may change us, but we start and end with the family.

—Anthony Brandt

ART, LIT, AND CREATIVITY

EVERYBODY IS A CONSUMER and enjoyer of creative works: the written word, visual arts, and performing arts. I'm guessing that quite a few people reading this book are also creators or performers of such works: poets, novelists, painters, illustrators, photographers, graphic designers, architects, musicians, dancers, crafters, chefs, tattooists, gingerbread house-makers (yes, I've met one who works at it full-time). . . . However we express ourselves, it's impossible not to wonder why and how we're doing it, not to mention whether we're doing it "well." Pretty much every creative person has wondered the same thing, and almost any famous one you can name has offered his or her thoughts. The quotes below probe creativity from both sides, as creator and as imbiber.

You think your pain and your heartbreak are unprecedented in the history of the world, but then you read. It was books that taught me that the things that tormented me most were the very things that connected me with all the people who were alive, or who had ever been alive.

—James Baldwin

Literature can train, and exercise, our ability to weep for those who are not us or ours. Who would we be if we could not sympathize with those who are not us or ours?

—Susan Sontag

A painting is a symbol for the universe. Inside it, each piece relates to the other. Each piece is only answerable to the rest of that little world. So, probably in the total universe, there is that kind of total harmony, but we get only little tastes of it. That's why people listen to music or look at paintings. To get in touch with that wholeness.

—Corita Kent

In every work of genius we recognize our own rejected thoughts; they come back to us with a certain alienated majesty.

—Ralph Waldo Emerson

Everything we think of as great has come to us from neurotics. It is they and they alone who found religions and create great works of art. The world will never realize how much it owes to them, and what they have suffered in order to bestow their gifts on it.

—Marcel Proust

Artists to my mind are the real architects of change, and not the political legislators who implement change after the fact.

—William S. Burroughs

If one is lucky, a solitary fantasy can totally transform one million realities.

—Maya Angelou

Do not read as children do, to enjoy themselves, or,
as the ambitious do, to educate themselves. No,
read to live.

   —Gustave Flaubert

Of all that is written, I love only what a person hath
written with his blood.

   —Friedrich Nietzsche

The test of literature is, I suppose, whether we ourselves
live more intensely for the reading of it.

   —Elizabeth Drew

Poetry heals the wounds
inflicted by reason.

—Novalis

Beneath the poetry of the texts, there is the actual
poetry, without form and without text.

—Antonin Artaud

Books say: She did this because. Life says: She did
this. Books are where things are explained to you; life
is where things aren't. I'm not surprised some people
prefer books.

—Julian Barnes

Life is a cornfield, but literature is that shot of whiskey that's been distilled down.

—Lorrie Moore

Read no history: nothing but biography, for that is life without theory.

—Benjamin Disraeli

Do not read so much; look about you and think of what you see there.

—Richard Feynman

Either write something worth reading or do something worth writing.

—Benjamin Franklin

Writing is a form of therapy; sometimes I wonder how all those who do not write, compose or paint can manage to escape the madness, the melancholia, the panic fear which is inherent in the human situation.

—Graham Greene

If you wish to be a writer,

write.

—Epictetus

In my writing I am acting as a map-maker, an explorer
of psychic areas . . . a cosmonaut of inner space, and I
see no point in exploring areas that have already been
thoroughly surveyed.

—William S. Burroughs

Somehow, poem-making and person-making
is the same thing.

—Li-Young Lee

Young man: May I kiss the hand that wrote *Ulysses*?

James Joyce: No, it did lots of other things, too.

Look, man, we'd probably most of us agree that these are dark times, and stupid ones, but do we need fiction that does nothing but dramatize how dark and stupid everything is? In dark times, the definition of good art would seem to be art that locates and applies CPR to those elements of what's human and magical that still live and glow despite the times' darkness. Really good fiction could have as dark a worldview as it wished, but it'd find a way both to depict this world and to illuminate the possibilities for being alive and human in it.

—David Foster Wallace

You don't have to write a book in order to reflect reality. You can also write a book to create reality.

—David Levithan

*I write because I don't know what I
think until I read what I say.*

—Flannery O'Connor

All in all, the creative act is not performed by the artist alone; the spectator brings the work in contact with the external world by deciphering and interpreting its inner qualification and thus adds his contribution to the creative act.

—Marcel Duchamp

I know what I have given you. I do not know what you have received.

—Antonio Porchia

At once it struck me what quality went to form a Man of Achievement, especially in Literature, and which Shakespeare possessed so enormously—I mean Negative Capability, that is, when a man is capable of being in uncertainties, mysteries, doubts, without any irritable reaching after fact and reason.

—John Keats

I used to think the function of art was the transformation of sorrow, but now I think it is the transformation of consciousness.

—Jane Miller

Art does not reproduce the visible; rather, it makes visible.

—Paul Klee

We've spent so much time judging what other people created that we've created very, very little of our own.

—Chuck Palahniuk

The act of making music, clothes, art, or even food has a very different, and possibly more beneficial effect on us than simply consuming those things. And yet for a very long time, the attitude of the state toward teaching and funding the arts has been in direct opposition to fostering creativity among the general population. It can often seem that those in power don't want us to enjoy making things for ourselves—they'd prefer to establish a cultural hierarchy that devalues our amateur efforts and encourages consumption rather than creation.

—David Byrne

Audience member at a lecture:
How do you become a prophet?

Allen Ginsberg:

Tell

your

secrets.

Extract the eternal from the ephemeral.

—Charles Baudelaire

A course on creativity in the arts and sciences, my
class attracted academic misfits of an enchanting sort.
Typically, a student might confess: "I'm in nuclear
physics, but my real passion is for medieval Irish song."

—Diane Ackerman

I invent nothing.
I rediscover.

—Auguste Rodin

The true artist will let his wife starve, his children go barefoot, his mother drudge for his living at seventy, sooner than work at anything but his art.

—George Bernard Shaw

It takes a lot of time to be a genius, you have to sit around so much doing nothing, really doing nothing.

—Gertrude Stein

Many of the greatest creations of man have been inspired by the desire to make money. When George Frederick Handel was on his beam ends, he shut himself up for twenty-one days and emerged with the complete score of *Messiah*—and hit the jackpot.

—David Mackenzie Ogilvy

To be a surrealist means barring from your mind all remembrance of what you have seen, and being always on the lookout for what has never been.

—René Magritte

Every child is an artist.
The problem is how to remain an artist
once he grows up.

—Pablo Picasso

Inside every man there is a poet who died young.

—Stefan Kanfer

An empty canvas is a living wonder—far lovelier than certain pictures.

—Wassily Kandinsky

If you hear a voice within you say, "You cannot paint," then by all means paint, and that voice will be silenced.

—Vincent van Gogh

It is known that Whistler when asked how long it took him to paint one of his nocturnes answered: "All of my life."

—Jorge Luis Borges

What I dream of is an art of balance, of purity and serenity devoid of troubling or depressing subject matter.

—Henri Matisse

I paint the light that emanates from all bodies.

—Egon Schiele

I found I could say things with colors and shapes that I couldn't say in any other way—things that I had no words for.

—Georgia O'Keeffe

Many say that life entered the human body by the help of music, but the truth is that life itself is music.

—Hafiz

After silence, that which comes nearest to expressing the inexpressible is music.

—Aldous Huxley

You've got to learn your instrument. Then, you practice, practice, practice. And then, when you finally get up there on the bandstand, forget all that and just wail.

—Charlie Parker

"Jazz" is a white term to define black people. My music is black classical music.

—Nina Simone

Dancing is the loftiest, the most moving, the most beautiful of the arts, because it is no mere translation or abstraction from life; it is life itself.

—Havelock Ellis

Ah, good taste! What a dreadful thing! Taste is the enemy of creativeness.

—Pablo Picasso

Follow your inner moonlight; don't hide the madness. You say what you want to say when you don't care who's listening.

—Allen Ginsberg

Creation is a drug I can't do without.

—Cecil B. DeMille

We consider the artist a special sort of person. It is more likely that each of us is a special sort of artist.

—Elsa Gidlow

AUTHORITY

GOVERNMENT, THE LEGAL SYSTEM, school, organized religions, the media, corporations, various economic concerns . . . there are a number of powerful, pervasive institutions that want to control you. It's either their overt purpose or a by-product of their very existence. In order to not disintegrate, they must have at least a piece of you, if not all of you, for at least part of your life, if not all of it. They might not have been created for nefarious purposes, but this is nonetheless the effect they often have. They flatten and deaden. They exploit and punish. They're never happy with the amount of power they have; they always seek to expand the breadth of their reach and the strength of their grip. This has not gone unnoticed by many of the finest and bravest minds throughout history. . . .

No man has any natural authority over his fellow men.

—Jean-Jacques Rousseau

Re-examine all you have been
told at school or church or
in any book, dismiss whatever
insults your own soul.

—Walt Whitman

I must Create a System, or be enslav'd by another Man's.

—William Blake

You never change things by fighting the existing reality. To change something, build a new model that makes the existing model obsolete.

—R. Buckminster Fuller

Do not wait for leaders; do it alone, person to person.

—Mother Teresa

The whole history of the progress of human liberty shows that all concessions yet made to her august claims have been born of earnest struggle. . . . If there is no struggle, there is no progress. Those who profess to favor freedom, and yet depreciate agitation, are men who want crops without plowing up the ground. They want rain without thunder and lightning. They want the ocean without the awful roar of its many waters. This struggle may be a moral one; or it may be a physical one; or it may be both moral and physical; but it must be a struggle. Power concedes nothing without a demand. It never did and it never will. Find out just what any people will submit to, and you have found out the exact amount of injustice and wrong which will be imposed upon them; and these will continue till they are resisted with either words or blows, or with both. The limits of tyrants are prescribed by the endurance of those whom they oppress.

—Frederick Douglass

It is better to die on your feet than live on your knees.

—Dolores Ibárruri

No matter what your fight, don't be ladylike! God Almighty made women, and the Rockefeller gang of thieves made the ladies.

—Mary Harris "Mother" Jones

Power tends to corrupt, and absolute power corrupts absolutely. Great men are almost always bad men . . .

—Lord Acton

It is honorable to be accused by those who deserve to be accused.

—Latin proverb

None are more hopelessly enslaved than those who falsely believe they are free.

—Johann Wolfgang von Goethe

To be governed is to be watched over, inspected, spied on, directed, legislated at, regulated, docketed, indoctrinated, preached at, controlled, assessed, weighed, censored, ordered about, by men who have neither the right, nor the knowledge, nor the virtue to do so. To be governed is to be at every operation, at every transaction, noted, registered, enrolled, taxed, stamped, measured, numbered, assessed, licensed, authorized, admonished, forbidden, reformed, corrected, punished. It is, under the pretext of public utility, and in the name of the general interest, to be placed under contribution, trained, ransomed, exploited, monopolized, extorted, squeezed, mystified, robbed; then, at the slightest resistance, the first word of complaint, to be repressed, fined, despised, harassed, tracked, abused, clubbed, disarmed, choked, imprisoned, judged, condemned, shot, deported, sacrificed, sold, betrayed; and, to crown all, mocked, ridiculed, outraged, dishonored. That is government; that is its justice; that is its morality.

—Pierre-Joseph Proudhon

When one has been threatened with a great
injustice, one accepts a smaller as a favour.

—Jane Carlyle

These laws of yours are no different from spiders' webs. They'll restrain anyone weak and insignificant who gets caught in them, but they'll be torn to shreds by people with power and wealth.

—Anacharsis

The law was made for one thing alone, for the exploitation of those who don't understand it, or are prevented by naked misery from obeying it.

—Bertolt Brecht

The more laws, the more offenders.

—Thomas Fuller

The degree of civilization in a society can be judged by entering its prisons.

—Fyodor Dostoevsky

Whenever the offence inspires less horror than the punishment, the rigor of penal law is obliged to give way to the common feelings of mankind.

—Edward Gibbon

Distrust all in whom the impulse to punish is powerful. . . . Distrust all those who talk much of their justice.

—Friedrich Nietzsche

It is fairly obvious that those who favor the death penalty have more affinity with assassins than those who do not.

—Remy de Gourmont

All Crimes are safe, but hated Poverty.
This, only this, the rigid Law pursues.

—Samuel Johnson

Mendoza: I am a brigand: I live by robbing the rich.

Tanner: I am a gentleman: I live by robbing the poor.

—George Bernard Shaw

In its majestic equality, the law forbids rich and poor alike to sleep under bridges, beg in the streets, and steal loaves of bread.

—Anatole France

When I give food to the poor, they call me a saint. When I ask why the poor have no food, they call me a communist.

—Archbishop Hélder Câmara

There is something wrong with the creation of this world, because the rich people think that they are the benefactors of the poor, but in fact those rich are fed and dressed by the work of these poor and live in luxury created for them by the poor.

—Leo Tolstoy

Growth for the sake of growth *is* the ideology of the cancer cell.

—Edward Abbey

In a consumer society there are inevitably two kinds of slaves: the prisoners of addiction and the prisoners of envy.

—Ivan Illich

Advertising has us chasing cars and clothes, working jobs we hate so we can buy **shit we don't need**.

—Chuck Palahniuk

The material on TV is called "programming" for a reason; it's designed to program us as we sit passively in our seat.

—Douglas Rushkoff

Puritanism:

The haunting fear that someone, somewhere, may be happy.

—H. L. Mencken

Moral indignation is jealousy **with a halo**.

—H. G. Wells

Why is the decision by a woman to sleep with a man she has just met in a bar a private one, and the decision to sleep with the same man for $100 subject to criminal penalties?

—Anna Quindlen

If men could get pregnant, abortion would be a sacrament.

—Florynce Kennedy

If the words "life, liberty, and the pursuit of happiness" don't include the right to experiment with your own consciousness, then the Declaration of Independence isn't worth the hemp it was written on.

—Terence McKenna

Outlawing drugs in order to solve drug problems is much like outlawing sex in order to win the war against AIDS.

—Ronald K. Siegel

No drug, not even alcohol, causes the fundamental ills of society. If we're looking for the source of our troubles, we shouldn't test people for drugs, we should test them for stupidity, ignorance, greed and love of power.

—P. J. O'Rourke

There is no history of mankind,
there are only many histories of all
kinds of aspects of human life.
And one of these is the history of
political power. This is elevated into
the history of the world.

—Karl Popper

What is politics, after all, but the compulsion to preside over property and make other peoples' decisions for them?

—Tom Robbins

Can anything be more ridiculous than that a man should have the right to kill me because he lives on the other side of the water, and because his ruler has a quarrel with mine, though I have none with him?

—Blaise Pascal

Democracy is the theory that the common people know what they want, and deserve to get it good and hard.

—H. L. Mencken

The best argument against democracy is a five-minute conversation with the average voter.

—Winston Churchill

Every government is run by liars, and nothing they say should be believed.

—I. F. Stone

A professional politician is a professionally dishonorable man. In order to get anywhere near high office he has to make so many compromises and submit to so many humiliations that he becomes indistinguishable from a streetwalker.

—H. L. Mencken

Unhappy the land that is in need of heroes.

—Bertolt Brecht

Every society honors its live conformists and its dead troublemakers.

—Mignon McLaughlin

The stuff they teach you at school is just
so they can own you.

—David Guterson

The only thing that interferes with my learning is my
education.

—Albert Einstein

I like quoting Einstein. Know why? Because nobody
dares contradict you.

—Studs Terkel

Nobody *gives* you an education. If you want one, you have to take it.

—John Taylor Gatto

It's not that I feel that school is a good idea gone wrong, but a wrong idea from the word go. It's a nutty notion that we can have a place where nothing but learning happens, cut off from the rest of life.

—John Holt

Self-education is, I firmly believe, the only kind of education there is.

—Isaac Asimov

If we taught babies to talk as most skills are taught in school, they would memorize lists of sounds in a predetermined order and practice them alone in a closet.

—Linda Darling-Hammond

As far as I have seen, at school as well as at home they aimed at blotting out one's individuality.

—Franz Kafka

Thank goodness I was never sent to school; it would have rubbed off some of the originality.

—Beatrix Potter

Children who live surrounded by rules, instead of learning about principles, end up becoming adept at getting around rules, finding the loopholes in rules, disguising non-compliance, or deflecting blame for non-compliance (i.e. lying about what they did). These are the skills that they then bring into adult life.

—Robyn Coburn

All the time you are in school, you learn through experience how to live in a dictatorship.

—Grace Llewellyn

How is it that little children are so intelligent and men so stupid? It must be education that does it.

—Alexandre Dumas

**Religions get lost
as people do.**

—Franz Kafka

Religions are intermittently too interesting, wise, and consoling to be abandoned to "believers" alone.

—*The Philosophers' Mail*

Such religion as there can be in modern life, every individual will have to salvage from the churches for himself.

—Lin Yutang

The language of religion is divisive partly because it tries to state what cannot be stated.

—William Stafford

And what would our ideas of God, of religion, be like if they had come to us through the minds of women? Ever think of that?

—Tom Robbins

THE BIG PICTURE

AT FIRST, THIS SMALL FINAL SECTION was meant as a catchall, a miscellany to hold the quotes that didn't belong anywhere else or couldn't be shoehorned into another section. Then I noticed that there is a theme, although it's hard to label. Maybe it's the big picture. All of these thoughts encompass the world, either in an abstract way—as in human existence, our collective lives on this planet, the march of history—or in a more literal way: the physical planet itself.

All the political, social, and economic improvements, all the technical progress cannot have any regenerating significance, so long as our inner life remains as it is at present. The more the intelligence unveils and violates the secrets of Nature, the more the danger increases and the heart shrinks.

—Nikos Kazantzakis

Actually, there are countless ways to live upon this tremorous sphere in mirth and good health, and probably only one way—the industrialized, urbanized, herding way—to live here stupidly, and man has hit upon that one wrong way.

—Tom Robbins

Any intelligent fool can make things bigger, more complex, and more violent. It takes a touch of genius— and a lot of courage—to move in the opposite direction.

—E. F. Schumacher

No theory, no ready-made system, no book that has ever been written will save the world. I cleave to no system. I am a true seeker.

—Michael Bakunin

That men do not learn very much from the lessons of history is the most important of all the lessons that history has to teach.

—Aldous Huxley

All really great things are happening in slow and inconspicuous ways.

—Leo Tolstoy

The sun, with all those planets revolving around it and dependent on it, can still ripen a bunch of grapes as if it had nothing else in the universe to do.

—Galileo Galilei

There are no passengers on spaceship earth.
We are all crew.

—Marshall McLuhan

My work is loving the world.

—Mary Oliver

ABOUT THE EDITOR

RUSS KICK is known for his groundbreaking and uniquely informative books, which have sold over half a million copies. He is the editor of the three-volume anthology *The Graphic Canon: The World's Greatest Literature as Comics and Visuals* (Seven Stories Press). NPR said it is "easily the most ambitious and successfully realized literary project in recent memory," *School Library Journal* called it "startlingly brilliant" and "a masterpiece," and *Booklist* declared it "a profound work of art." The third volume was a *New York Times* bestseller.

Russ has also edited megaselling anthologies *You Are Being Lied To* and *Everything You Know Is Wrong*, and has written several nonfiction books, including the cult classic *50 Things You're Not Supposed to Know* (all from Disinformation Books). The *New York Times* has dubbed him "an information archaeologist," *Details* magazine described him as "a Renaissance man," and *Utne Reader* named him one of its "50 Visionaries Who Are Changing Your World."

ACKNOWLEDGMENTS

THANKS GO TO my mom and my sister. My Chicago family. All my friends.

This book has been percolating in the back of my brain for years, and I'm grateful to Jan Johnson, Michael Kerber, and Gary Baddeley for letting me make it happen. Thanks also to Kim Ehart, Bonni Hamilton, Sylvia Hopkins, Matt Staggs, and everyone else at Red Wheel/Weiser and Disinfo.

A tip of the hat to everyone who told me their favorite quotes, including Erika Roush, Laura Folkwein, Eran Levin, Brooke Anderson, Will Cordeiro, Cybele Knowles, Bryan Kromenacker, Jan, Gary, and Kim. Merci beaucoup to fellow quote-mongers Sy Safransky of *The Sun,* Maria Popova of BrainPickings.org, Lewis Lapham of *Lapham's Quarterly*, Wikiquote, and, of course, John Bartlett.

Major thanks are due to everyone who makes the printed Flash Wisdom and gets it into your hands: the paper-makers, the truck drivers, the printers, the distributors and wholesalers, the booksellers. . . . And of course the many trees who gave their all.

Most crucial of all: An endlessly deep debt of gratitude to every person quoted in these pages.